MOMMY, WHO IS MALCOLM X?

AARON D. WHEATLEY

Copyright © 2024 Aaron D. Wheatley
All rights reserved.
ISBN: 979-8-87860-611-0 paperback

This novel comes to life in the warm glow of countless shared stories and the entrancing shine of goodnight stars. "Mommy, Who Is Malcolm X?" is dedicated to the many young hearts just like yours as well as to you, my bright-eyed adventurer.

I hope this tale takes the reader on a trip through bravery, justice, and history. May you find within you the strength to stand up for what is right, the power of understanding, and the wisdom of turning these pages.

I hope Malcolm X's story encourages you to have ambitious dreams, ask fearless questions, and appreciate the beauty of diversity and unity. This dedication serves as a reminder that, like Malcolm X, you have the power to alter the world through your compassion and curiosity.

With love and endless aspirations,

Aaron D. Wheatley

MOMMY, WHO IS MALCOLM X?

Copyright © 2024 Aaron D. Wheatley

The right of Aaron D. Wheatley to be identified as the Author of the work has been asserted by him in accordance with the Copyright, Designs and Patents Act 1988

All rights reserved. Printed in the United States of America. No part of this publication may be stored in a retrieval system, transmitted, used or reproduced in any manner whatsoever without written permission except in the case of brief quotations embodied in critical articles or reviews, without permission of the publisher, nor be otherwise circulated in any form of binding or cover other than that in which it is published and without a similar condition being imposed on the subsequent purchaser. This book is a work of fiction. Names, characters, businesses, organizations, places, events and incidents are either the product of the author's imagination or are used fictitiously. Any resemblance to actual persons, living or dead, events, or locales is entirely coincidental.

Contact Info: www.SpookyTalesNetwork.com
Front Cover Design by: Aaron D. Wheatley
Hard Cover Wrap Design by: Aaron D. Wheatley
Editor: Aaron D. Wheatley
Illustrator: Aaron D. Wheatley
ISBN: 979-8-87860-611-0 paperback
First Edition: February 2024

MOMMY, WHO IS MALCOLM X?

AARON D. WHEATLEY

Copyright © 2024 Aaron D. Wheatley
All rights reserved.
ISBN: 979-8-87363-468-2 paperback

SIGN UP FOR MY
AUTHOR NEWSLETTER

Follow me on social media to stay up to date with my writing.

Be the first to learn about Aaron D. Wheatley's new releases and receive exclusive content for both readers and writer!

WWW.SPOOKYTALESNETWORK.COM

NeutronTheGod@gmail.com

Instagram: @SpookyTalesNetwork

Facebook: @SpookyTalesNetwork

TiKTok: @SpookyTalesNetwork

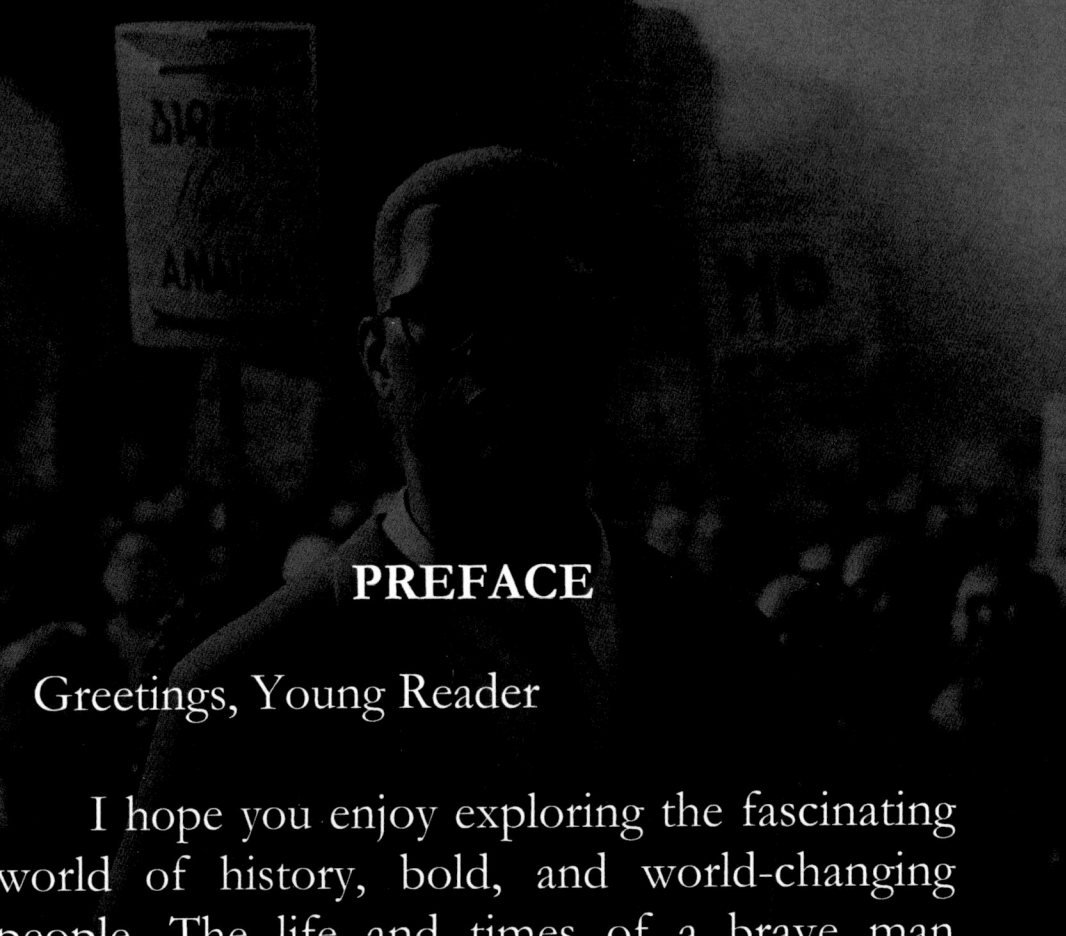

PREFACE

Greetings, Young Reader

I hope you enjoy exploring the fascinating world of history, bold, and world-changing people. The life and times of a brave man named Malcolm X are documented in these pages. Here we can learn from his experiences about courage, ability to adapt, and the endless quest of justice.

Beyond just a tale, "Mommy, Who Is Malcolm X?" is a historical adventure that teaches values of unity and standing up for what is right. Discover Malcolm X's life through this book. He was born into a society that did not value fairness, especially for people who resembled him.

You will go along with Maya, a curious and intelligent young girl, as she learns about the life of Malcolm X. You will learn about his hardships, his aspirations, and the inspirational message he shared with the world, through vivid narration and heartwarming images.

By treating everyone with love and respect, we can all make a difference, even in the face of adversity, as Malcolm X's narrative serves as a reminder.

I hope that Malcolm X's bravery, his faith in justice, and his hope for a better world will inspire you as you turn the pages and begin this journey, dear reader.

Sincerely,

Aaron D. Wheatley

In a cozy room glowing softly with bedtime stars, Maya's eyes sparkled with curiosity as she turned to her mother, a question tugging at her heart. "Mommy, who is Malcolm X?"

Her mother settled beside her, ready to share the story of a brave hero who stood up for what's right, determined to change the world.

"Malcolm X was an amazing person, Maya. He was like a superhero for fairness" her mother said, her voice carrying the magic of history.

Maya's imagination ran wild as her mother described Malcolm X's childhood while she cuddled up. Malcolm Little was born in Omaha, Nebraska, on May 19, 1925.

"He was born a long time ago, when things weren't fair for everyone, especially for those like him with beautiful dark skin," her mother said. Due to the color of his skin, he experienced injustice. Life was difficult for his family because of the meanness that certain people encountered.

"However, Malcolm X even as a kid, fought through difficult times," her mother added. "He believed everyone should be treated fairly, no matter what they looked like." He discussed the value of equal opportunities for all people in life.

"He wanted everyone to work together, like one big team, to make the world a better place," she said. Maya saw the value of sticking up for what's right even when it's difficult.

Maya's mind danced as her mother explained how Malcolm X gained valuable knowledge while locked up in jail. "He discovered books that changed his life."

Her mother went on, "Malcolm X was extremely smart and powerful." Despite his difficult circumstances, he became aware of the Nation of Islam.

According to her mother, they were strong in unity and fought for justice, particularly for African Americans. Malcolm was so proud of his background and of their views that he took on the last name X.

Malcolm X rose to fame in the Nation of Islam after being released from prison, similar to a superhero. Malcolm X gained popularity with his speeches that aligned with people who wanted justice and to be proud of their identity, almost like music.

He spoke in a way that sparked strong emotions in listeners and got them to consider treating one another with kindness. "With a strong voice for justice and respect, he worked to help African Americans.

No matter how someone looked, Malcolm X wanted everyone to be friends," her mother clarified. "He learned that we're all the same inside, no matter the color of our skin."

But there are obstacles for even superheroes. Some people were offended by Malcolm X's desire for equal treatment for all.

Conflicts with his group and its leader, Elijah Muhammad, occasionally resulted from his ideas upsetting some people.

He had to walk away from the Nation of Islam after a number of arguments. Malcolm X, however, gained knowledge and proposed rather than complaining.

Her mother went on, "In 1964, Malcolm X went on a trip far away to a special place called Mecca," her words creating a picture of equality.

He witnessed people of all colors praying together there, and it gave him the impression that everyone, regardless of background, deserves to be treated with kindness.

Her mother softly remarked, "But Maya, Malcolm X's journey had a sad part too." Malcolm X was harmed by people who failed to understand his magic words on February 21, 1965, while he was in New York City speaking with friends.

Malcolm X died as a result. For anybody who wished for kindness and justice in the world, it was an extremely depressing day. His story didn't finish there, but it was like an awful end to a book.

Her mother gently said, "Even though Malcolm X isn't here anymore, his words and ideas still inspire people today. He wanted everyone to be like superheroes, standing up for fairness and being proud of who they are."

Maya felt, like a real-life superhero, the warmth of Malcolm X's bravery and the importance of standing up for justice and kindness as she curled up under her blanket.

Maya was left with visions of a society in which everyone might be a hero for justice after Malcolm X's story was transformed into a magical story.

A tale of justice, fairness, kindness, bravery, and the hope that one day everyone will be treated equally, with respect and love, as he desired.

Maya's mother said softly, "Malcolm X left behind a big lesson for us. He showed us that even when things are tough, we can stand up for fairness and make the world a better place."

With a mixture of regret and respect for Malcolm X's courage, Maya nodded. Just by speaking out for justice and kindness, even one person can make a great impact, as her mother told her as she tucked her in.

SIGN UP FOR MY AUTHOR NEWSLETTER

Follow me on social media to stay up to date with my writing.
Be the first to learn about Aaron D. Wheatley's new releases and receive exclusive content for both readers and writer!

WWW.SPOOKYTALESNETWORK.COM
NeutronTheGod@gmail.com
Instagram: @SpookyTalesNetwork
Facebook: @SpookyTalesNetwork
TiKTok: @SpookyTalesNetwork

Made in the USA
Las Vegas, NV
15 February 2025

18204804R00026